How to be
RESILIENT

What others are saying about *"How To Be Resilient"*

"This wonderful, warm, inspiring book shows you how to overcome any obstacle, and bounce back from every setback. It can change your philosophy of life."

~Brian Tracy – Author,
The Power of Self-Confidence

"In a world that is becoming more focused on fear, division and living through the media rather than through one's authentic self and purpose, Stacey shines a clear light on how to rediscover a world of gratitude and wonder with life. Grab hold of your life by grabbing this book. Refreshing, inviting and uplifting."

~ *Jeffrey* Slayter - International Best Selling Author, Entrepreneur, and Speaker

"Stacey has de-codified the art of human happiness in providing a roadmap for the greatest quest of all, overcoming adversity. In speaking from her own experience of the ultimate human trial, Stacey holds your hand on your own personal journey to happiness."

~ Jack Delosa,
founder of The Entourage
& BRW Young Rich List Member

"Stacey Copas is a resilient young lady. Her book not only is written from her experience but it is a practical and inspirational, heartfelt story. From tragedy to triumph, to an absolute winner. It truly is a blueprint for getting results."

~Pat Mesiti - Entrepreneur,
International Bestselling Author,
Speaker and Mindset Expert

"Becoming the most successful surfer in history and paving the way for future generations required me to adapt to the ebbs and flows of life and its challenges. Adversity and setbacks tested my character, hunger, work ethic and my resilience. If you want to know how to use resilience to accelerate your success, you must read this book."

~ Layne Beachley AO,
7 times world surfing champion,
motivational speaker
and founder and director of the
Aim For The Stars Foundation

© Stacey Copas 2015

All rights reserved.

No part of this book may be reproduced or transmitted in any form or by any means, electronic or mechanical, including photocopying, recording or by any information storage and retrieval system, without written permission from the author, except for the inclusion of brief quotations in a review.

Every effort has been made to ensure this book is free from error or omissions. However, the Publisher, the Author, the Editor, or their respective employees or agents, shall not accept responsibility for injury, loss or damage occasioned to any person acting or refraining from action as a result of material in this book, whether or not such an injury, loss or damage is in any way due to any negligent act or omission, breach of duty or default on the part of the Publisher, the Author, their respective employees or agents
.

1st Edition published in 2015 by
Resilience For Results
Adelaide, Australia

Web: www.resilienceforresults.com

How To Be Resilient

Printed in Australia by Ingram Spark

Paperback 9 780646 940502

*"Be like water making its way through cracks.
Do not be assertive, but adjust to the object, and you
shall find a way round or through it.
If nothing within you stays rigid, outward
things will disclose themselves.*

*Empty your mind, be formless. Shapeless, like water.
If you put water into a cup, it becomes the cup.
You put water into a bottle and it becomes the bottle.
You put it in a teapot it becomes the teapot.
Now, water can flow or it can crash. Be water my friend."*

~ Bruce Lee

Acknowledgements

It has been a long, exciting and often challenging road bringing this book to you. Along the way there have been many people who have played part in my development, the fine tuning of my niche and message, and who have challenged me to get out of my own way and play a bigger game. Thank you Pat Mesiti, Jason Partington, Annette Lackovic, Jack Delosa and the legends at The Entourage, Judeth Wilson, Allan Pease, Joanna Martin, Mal Emery, Layne Beachley and Jeffrey Slayter.

To my amazing family, thanks for being such a well-balanced blend of challenge and support. You've allowed me to be myself, take risks and to spread my wings while being there for anything I needed. My best friend Jen Greenaway, thank you for being there for all of the ups and downs. You are my honesty barometer and call me out when I need it. Love you all.

Without Mike Jung this book would never have happened. Thank you so much for your love, support and encouragement to stretch myself beyond anything I could have imagined. You have always downplayed how much of an impact you have had in my life. No downplaying now, it is in print!

Massive thanks to the team behind the book. Guy Vincent, Jenny Hassam, Chris Martin, Leon Woods and Deanna Lang, you brought all the pieces together for me. Finally, thank you to the supporters of the crowdfunding campaign which gave me the "nudge" to finish this book, special thanks to Celine Egan, Andrea Davies, Amanda Horne, Corinne Namblard, Diana De Hulsters, Guy Vincent, Kristie Wieland, Jan and Don Milne, Kiara Cannizzaro, Lynda Kutek, Sarah Davies, Steve Shipley, Soula Dagas, Lesley Geldenhuys, Rob Wallis and Kurt Walter.

*This book is dedicated to the adversity that
has been part of my journey through life.
I am grateful for every piece of it
and the growth it has given me.
Adversity is my friend.*

Contents

Foreword 1

Introduction 3

What is resilience and why is it important? 11

How is this approach different? 15

Responsibility 19

Responsibility In Action 26

Excuses 29

Eliminating Excuses in Action 32

Support 35

Improvisation 45

Improvisation in Action 50

Language 53

Language in Action 60

Inspiration 63

Inspiration in Action 67

Expand	73
Expansion in Action	76
Next	79
Next in Action	84
Time	87
Time in Action	92
Bonus Principles	95
Confidence	97
Confidence in Action	102
Enjoyment	105
Enjoyment in Action	110
Summary	113
Next Steps	115
Recommended Reading	119
About The Author	121

Foreword

One of the most powerful traits any person can develop is that of resilience. Learning to become resilient will give you a solid foundation for achieving success in any area of your life because when things don't go according to plan, when you are being constantly challenged, disappointed and rejected, resilience is the difference between giving up and moving forward.

When I was diagnosed with cancer on three separate occasions I decided that whatever the outcome, I would be resilient and move forward to bigger and better things in my life, and that I would live to an old age.

At age 45, I made several poor business decisions and lost everything I had owned, and went from the penthouse to the outhouse almost overnight. After 2 years of depression and financial mayhem, I made the decision to return to financial independence and to always be able to have anything I ever wanted. Choosing to be resilient was the key.

Some people believe that resilience is something you either have or you do not. While it is true that some people do seem to have it naturally, it is definitely a trait that you can learn. This is why I was excited to hear that Stacey was writing this book. Stacey has been through her own adversity and huge personal challenges and has been able to document in this book the simple, practical principles that anyone can apply to developing their own resilience.

I first heard Stacey talk about resilience and overcoming adversity at a conference several years ago and I was inspired by her journey. When she asked me to contribute to this book I was keen because she has a unique story that shows what human resilience can overcome.

This book will show you the simple ideas and strategies for dealing with adversity in your life and moving forward to bigger and greater achievements.

Allan Pease

Author, Body Language

Introduction

I remember vividly the day my life changed forever. It was a hot Sunday afternoon in early December 1990 and I was 12 years old. My Dad was going to play indoor cricket and my younger brother and I had a choice of going to watch him play or going to a relative's place for a swim. Clearly no contest there!

Mum and Dad dropped us off for an afternoon of swimming with our cousins and headed off to the indoor cricket centre. We literally ran straight through the house to the pool, shedding our clothes as we got to the backyard ready to cool off. I remember being particularly excited to be wearing my new swimming costume – a very brightly coloured Ken Done print.

Not being content just splashing around with the other younger boys I climbed up on to the edge of the pool – an above ground pool with a narrow colour bond metal type edge on the sides – and dived into the shallow water. That was so much more fun. This didn't go unnoticed and I got yelled at to stop.

Being 12 years old, bulletproof and invincible, these warnings of potential harm went in one ear and out the other. Time after time I climbed up, steadied myself and dove into the cool water. I was unhappy with the way my legs flopped as I dived in so I climbed up on to the ledge once more, determined that this dive was going to be perfect.

I focused on keeping my legs together as I dove in and launched myself. It was very strange. I was not aware of anything going wrong but when I tried to swim to the surface like I had done every dive before this one I found that I could not move. I felt no pain but after a few seconds the panic set in.

I could see the other boys splashing around and I tried desperately to move. I held my breath as long as I could but panic took over. When I could not hold it any longer I gave in and took a breath and blacked out as my lungs filled with water. Eventually my brother realised something was wrong and pulled me out of the pool.

I was rushed by ambulance to the local hospital, and have vague recollections of fading in and out of consciousness on the way to the hospital. At the hospital I remember my precious swimming costume being cut from me and a buzz of people around.

Later that night after a helicopter airlift and another ambulance ride, I ended up in intensive care at Royal North Shore Hospital in Sydney. It was there that I was told that I had broken my neck and drowned and that I would never walk again. At that time it certainly was a devastating blow and the end of my life as I knew it. My initial thoughts were that I would prove them wrong.

I spent the next 8 weeks flat on my back with sandbags on either side of my head, watching TV using a mirror (I learned to read backwards watching Wheel of Fortune), and having someone turn the pages of books for me. I could not even feed myself. Instead of our usual family Christmas at home it was spent around my hospital bed.

Going from being fiercely independent and so active to being completely dependent on others for everything was soul destroying.

I was to spend 7 months in hospital and unfortunately, because of my age I missed out on a proper rehabilitation because the doctors said I was too young to go to the rehab centre where everyone else went after around 3 months in hospital following a similar injury. This meant I was sent home unable to dress myself, unable to go to the toilet without help and barely able to push myself in my wheelchair. To top it off, a few days after leaving hospital I started high school half way through the year, at a school far from home, where I knew no one. It felt like the Universe was really against me at that time. I was incredibly depressed and barely smiled, and I felt that I was a huge burden on my family.

Later that year I had the chance to spend a week at the rehab centre in my school holidays – funny how 12 was too young but 13 was ok? I ended up staying 3 weeks and the transformation in my ability in that time was remarkable. I went in totally dependent and came out almost independent.

It was the first big turning point for me to get some confidence in myself again and a desire to keep moving rather than questioning my existence. It also made me realise how much better I could have been with proper rehab in the beginning. This was where I shifted my focus to what I had rather than what I had lost.

Over the subsequent years, I was able to move to a school closer to home which helped greatly with how I was feeling about myself. It was a selective high school which meant that I was challenged academically for the first time since I had started high school. My younger brother started there at the same time as I did so it was reassuring to have him there to back me up if I needed it. I made friends pretty easily but this was largely because of some of the habits I had picked up along the way.

By 14 years old I was smoking, getting drunk and getting stoned regularly. This continued for another few years and it was my way of numbing the emotional pain I had from having my life turned upside down.

Eventually I realised that I was killing my brain as I was feeling foggier and foggier all the time. I was also experiencing deeper, darker depths of depression and anxiety when I was not drunk or stoned. I realised I had to make a change. I am proud to say that I have not smoked since high school and I had a period of 5 years post high school where I did not have a single drop of alcohol. More recently, I have made the decision to give up drinking completely. In hindsight this was an important step for me to start to deal with how torn up I was feeling about my life not being the way I had intended it back prior to the accident. I hid this very well from everyone.

Most people thought I was remarkable in getting on with my life the way I did, getting a job and having what appeared to outsiders to be a relatively normal life. Inside though, I was still hurting badly and at the lowest points contemplated checking out from what was my life.

The thought of ending up in worse shape than I was in was the only thing that drew me back from that dangerous liaison with the other side.

Fast forward many years on and I was to realise

that this event was actually going to change my life for the better. Most people find it hard to believe that ending up a quadriplegic and needing to use a wheelchair for the rest of my life is a positive thing but after spending some time with me they quickly realise that I am truly happy about it. I have done things with my life that I can say with certainty that I would never have done otherwise.

These days I have the most fulfilling life, a life I still sometimes find quite surreal. Not being able to walk or use my hands and arms fully has not held me back and some of my achievements to date include:-

- *Working full time in open employment since leaving school in a variety of roles in various sectors*

- *Running for parliament in the 2007 NSW State Elections. By the way, I no longer aspire to be a politician!*

- *Moving from Sydney to Adelaide where I knew no one other than Mike who is now my husband, had no job to go to, no support services and had never even been on a plane*

- *Buying several properties in the Adelaide Hills – the start of our empire*

- *Delivering life changing education to wheelchair users in the Solomon Islands; education that could prevent them from becoming one of 3/4 of people in developing countries that die within 2 years of suffering a spinal injury.*

- *Taking up athletics again and training for the 2016 Rio Paralympic Games after 22 years of avoiding sport following a pact with my 12 year old self to never play sport again*

- *And now sharing what I have learned through my life experiences and philosophies about resilience and finding the opportunities in change and adversity, in my role as a speaker, trainer, consultant, coach and author*

I do not share this to impress you but to highlight what is possible when even the worst things go wrong. On reflection, my parents must have had some hidden intuition when they named me, as Stacey comes from the Greek name Anastasia which means "resurrection" or "she who will rise again". How is that for a resilient name?

Having a brush with death and losing the ability to walk has meant that I take nothing for granted. Not only do I appreciate fully every day that I have, I now having a burning desire to see more, do more, give more and be more. I would love nothing more than to ignite that desire in other people, to teach people how to be resilient, and get results even when things don't go according to plan.

So how did I get from where I was to where I am now? I took some time to reflect on how it happened – some of it consciously and some unconsciously – and have reverse engineered how I was able to do that. In this book I am going to share with you the key principles that I believe have been the driving force behind my success and can be the key principles that can get you the results you desire too if you implement them into your life. A standout in these keys is in the area of support.

It has been a huge turning point for me having people in my life that believed in me more than I believed in myself. These people who I class as my mentors and cheerleaders saw something in me well before I saw it. They have been able to dispel any doubts, prejudices or fears I had about sharing my story and got me to realise that my experiences, good and bad, and the lessons I have learned in the process could have a profound impact in the lives of others. My experiences as a speaker and trainer to date have proved that they were overwhelmingly correct!

Now that I am sharing these key principles that have given me the resilience to turn what was a tragedy at the time into the successful life I have now, it is my turn to be able to be the person, the mentor and the cheerleader, that believes in others more than they believe in themselves. Some of you may get that by just applying these principles directly from this blueprint and others may wish to work with me personally to guide you through implementing them into you own life. Either way I am excited and proud to share these principles with you, and to play some part in your own development to becoming more resilient.

Enjoy the blueprint and be sure to share your thoughts, insights, feedback and challenges with me at

Stacey@HowToBeResilient.com.

What is resilience and why is it important?

There are varying definitions of resilience and even more interpretations of what it means from person to person. The dictionary defines resilience as "the ability to recover or return to an original form after being bent, compressed or stretched, or the ability to recover readily from illness, depression, adversity or the like".

I believe that it is more than just recovering or returning to an original form. I believe it is the ability to go further than you were before you were faced with the challenge that required your resilience to overcome it. It is an opportunity to grow, learn and adapt, to actually leverage the challenge and adversity into a more positive outcome.

Have you ever noticed how some people appear to be unflappable when even major things go wrong whereas other people fall to pieces? Resilience is this ability to keep it together when faced with a problem or a setback when others would fall apart. It is the ability and strength to cope when things don't go according to plan.

It does not remove stress or problems. It means that people with resilience are able to deal with the problems, to take on the challenges and get on with things.

There is often a perception that resilience is something you either have naturally or you do not. The reality is that resilience is a skill that can be learned and just like building muscle in the gym, the more you practise it, the more resilient you will become. Another way to visualise this is to think of jumping on a trampoline – the lower down it goes the higher up you are launched.

Resilience is a critical tool to have in your arsenal as it will give you the ability to follow through on everything you set out to do. This could be as simple as getting through the day or as complex as achieving a lifelong dream or goal. Resilience when looking at being successful in business and life in general is especially important as most people call it quits the first time things don't go according to plan.

We all know that the path to achieving a goal or dream is littered with obstacles and most people give up as soon as something goes wrong. Being a resilient person means that you will be able to achieve your goals no matter how many things go wrong or the magnitude of the things going wrong along the way.

An additional benefit of becoming more and more resilient is when things go amiss you begin to look at it in an entirely different light. You will start to see opportunities instead of problems and it can spawn a whole new train of thought you would not have encountered. It can stimulate your creativity.

The more resilient I become personally, the more I look forward to looking at the challenges square in the face, almost taunting them, as I know overcoming these challenges fuels my desire to achieve my goals even more and set even bigger goals.

*"Anyone can give up,
it's the easiest thing in the world to do.
But to hold it together when everyone else
would understand if you fell apart,
that's true strength."*

How is this approach different?

Most books, training and information in the marketplace on resilience focus on resilience from a psychological or academic point of view. There is nothing wrong with this approach at all, however I find the psychological approach places its emphasis on just coping with the stress of a mishap, which I consider a shortcoming

Other materials that are more academic and jargon filled can come across as being complicated or difficult to implement. These principles are incredibly practical and most can be implemented on the spot with just a decision to do so.

Many of the clients I have worked with over the years were relieved to hear that my approach is practical and tied to my personal narrative, using storytelling as it "clicked" better and gained more traction, much faster.

This blueprint is focused strongly on getting the results you desire not just feeling better about being thrown off course. I don't know about you but I cannot think of any greater way to feel better about things going amiss than to actually achieve the goal you were working towards when you got hit with the problem. Think about how amazing it will be to soak up the feeling of success having achieved your goal despite all of the dramas you faced along the way?

Using the principles outlined in this book, you will be able to get to the place where you can experience that amazing feeling of triumph made even sweeter by the fact that you slayed a few dragons in the process.

This is not a step by step process to follow. It is a collection of key principles that you can use as you would a conventional toolkit. Different tools are required for different jobs and sometimes more than one tool is required to complete a job.

A quick caveat before we begin. These principles sound simple and that is because they are simple. Do not fall into the trap of saying to yourself, "yeah I know that." Instead ask yourself, "am I doing that?" Would you agree that there is a huge difference between knowing something and actually doing it? While taking in each principle take the time to capture your thoughts as you go. There are large margins to give you plenty of space to write so make use of the space. This book is designed to be more of a manual than a read and put back on the shelf type of book. If you would prefer not to write in the book, you can download a PDF activity book with all of the exercises at: www.howtoberesilient.com/resources

Responsibility

The 8 weeks I spent on bed rest flat on my back following my accident were the toughest 8 weeks of my life. Being immobile for so long and being a young person meant that I had a massive growth spurt. I added close to 4 inches in a short period of time! This would have been very cool if I was on my feet and able to show it off but unfortunately because I was not on my feet, and weight bearing, calcium started to leave my bones and make its way into my bloodstream. I had no idea any of this was happening until I started vomiting endlessly. Being flat on my back and unable to turn my head made this an incredibly unpleasant experience. I could not keep anything down and being exhausted, frustrated and humiliated by being so helpless and sick I was desperate for it to stop.

It was then I decided that it was pointless taking the handfuls of tablets I was being subjected to. What was the point? I was going to throw them up anyway. Waste of their tablets and an unpleasant experience for me. Unfortunately, the medical team did not agree with me and they called in a child psychologist to tell me that they were the doctors and I was not. Pardon the pun but I did not take it lying down! I debated endlessly with them and eventually caved in and resumed the ritual of gulping down the tablets. What changed though was that it made me even more determined to have some control in a situation where all control had been taken from me.

*"The day you take
complete responsibility for yourself,
the day you stop making any excuses
- that's the day you start to the top."*

My new approach was that I interrogated the medical team every time I saw them wanting to know the ins and outs, ups and downs and every possible alternative to the treatments they prescribed. I refused to take anything without reading the medication guide first and I generally gave them hell. In their eyes I was probably a pain in the backside, obnoxious kid, but in hindsight I was taking responsibility for my own wellbeing and seeking the best possible outcomes I could. This approach of questioning everything to find the full spectrum of options available in every situation has stayed with me and has served me exceptionally well.

The issue of responsibility is the most important – and potentially the hardest – to address. When things go wrong the first thing most people do is look for someone or something to blame. Taking responsibility does not necessarily always mean putting your hand up and saying "yes, I stuffed up" or "yes, it was my fault" regardless of the situation.

Quite often things going wrong can be the direct result of something you have done or a decision you have made. In that situation, the best thing to do is to admit it and keep moving. This is taking responsibility. It is not being at fault. There is a difference. There is nothing worse than when people do not accept responsibility for their own actions. I have heard people like that referred to as having a disease called "Blame-a-titis". Make sure you protect yourself from catching it!

Even when the situation is something completely out of your control it is better to accept responsibility for finding the solution rather than blaming someone else for the problem. All blaming does is give more power to something that will have a negative impact in your life. It is actually giving away your personal power and control, over time it creates a victim mentality.

In my life I would have ended up a bitter mess if I had not taken responsibility for the actions that have left me needing a wheelchair for the rest of my life and for making something of my life. I admit it was something that did not happen overnight but if I had not, I certainly would not be sharing with you today!

When I realised that the experience I have is completely in my hands, my life changed. You see no one can "make" you feel, do or say anything. No matter what is happening around you, none of it is happening "to you". You have total responsibility for your reaction to external stimulus and your interaction with it.

What that means is whether an experience is positive or negative is your choice.

In a business environment, change is constant and it is one of the most frequent challenges you will come up against and need resilience for. Some of the change comes from the marketplace and is external and some comes internally – often as a response to those external changes. Change in business generally comes from a place of good intention. No one decides to make change to upset people or to make their lives difficult. These decisions are made for an overall positive impact, even if it feels negative in the short term.

Take responsibility and look for the opportunity created by change. Start with exploring how you can contribute ideas and suggestions to make improvements within your sphere of influence – be that in your personal life or the organisation you are a part of, and find ways to shape the process of change. Too often people feel that they do not have the power to make a difference. We all do. Some people's circles of influence are just wider reaching than others. The more you look for ways to add value to your circle of influence, the wider reaching it will become.

By taking responsibility for your reaction to change you are contributing to a more positive impact rather than simply being a passenger and feeling frustrated and helpless.

I have learned a lot along my journey and it has set me up in life to take responsibility for myself rather than just letting others decide what was best for me. By doing so I have put myself in the driver's seat of my life rather than being a passenger. Take a moment to ask yourself which seat are you sitting in for your own life?

Taking personal responsibility begins with making a decision to do so. It is as simple as seeing something in your life you are dissatisfied with and deciding that you want something better. You do not have to know exactly what you would like nor how you will get it. That will come. No matter how bad things are you have the chance to decide you want something better for your life. Do not give away that power!

*"You must take personal responsibility.
You cannot change the circumstances, the seasons,
or the wind, but you can change yourself.
That is something you have charge of."*
– Jim Rohn

Responsibility In Action

On a scale of 1-10 (1 being very poor and 10 being outstanding) how do you rate the level of responsibility you currently take immediately after something goes wrong?

List any areas of your life where you need to improve your level of responsibility.

Questions to prompt if this is not evident immediately:

- *In my life I feel I have no choice about……*

- *In my life I feel I have no control over……*

Create 3 questions you can ask yourself to help you improve your ability to take personal responsibility.

e.g: Why is it so easy for me to take responsibility for the experiences I have?

Excuses

As far as I am concerned "Constantly making excuses simply means you do not want to succeed". I know it sounds harsh but think about the people that you know who constantly make excuses and complain? Then think about how many of those people you would class as successful and happy? Making excuses is lying to yourself and it takes a whole load of energy to do. This energy is far better spent on finding solutions to the jam you are in.

> *"If you really want to do something, you'll find a way. If you don't, you'll find an excuse."*
> *– Jim Rohn*

The realisation that constantly making excuses was lying to myself and killing my chances of success was a massive wake up call. I had a really bad habit of being late to just about everything and making excuses for being late. A classic excuse was something along the lines of "it took me much longer to get ready than I thought it would." This was an excuse that most people just accepted since they have no idea how long it takes for someone who uses a wheelchair to get ready to go out. I did this for most of my life.

It was not until I was at a seminar a few years back and the presenter was talking about the traits of successful people. He hammered home how important punctuality was. As he spoke initially I was still justifying my tardiness to myself. That was until he said "being late shows a lack of respect for the people you have an appointment with and a lack of respect for their time." Boom! That hit me so hard. I had never stopped to think about the impact of being late but it was more than just the lateness issue that got me thinking.

Not only was I being disrespectful, I was doing myself a massive disservice by making excuses about being late when the reality was I was being lazy and disorganised by not allowing myself enough time. For the most part I felt bad every time I did it but it took that one line in a seminar to break me out of the habit and resolve to not only be a punctual person but to actually be early.

Over the years of coaching people one-on-one I have probably heard every excuse under the sun. It still surprises me at times that people will invest a lot of money into coaching but still retain their "Excusiologist" traits almost as if that by investing a lot of money their challenges will magically disappear. The reality is that challenges only disappear when you start to dig deep into the root cause of the excuses and flip them on their head.

Instead of excuses why not to do things (usually a long list of all of the things that might go wrong) start to make a list of all of the reasons it will go well. Turning excuses why not into positive reasons why is a great way to make things go well! There is an exercise at the end of this section that will help you to uncover the deeper reasons behind some of the excuses you may be hiding behind that are holding you back from success. When you find yourself about to make an excuse, stop and think about the impact of that excuse. It is very easy to say that you did not get something completed because of an unexpected problem but think about how that will be viewed by someone else. Stop for a moment and ask yourself, if one of your friends gave that excuse how would you feel? Think about how you feel about saying it, especially if you had not done everything you possibly could to complete your task regardless of something going wrong. Could this be a lie to yourself? Be 100% accountable to yourself and you will get results despite the challenges.

"People spend too much time finding other people to blame, too much energy finding excuses for not being what they are capable of being, and not enough energy putting themselves on the line, growing out of the past, and getting on with their lives."
- J Michael Straczynski

Eliminating Excuses in Action

Are there things you frequently use as excuses? List them below.

_____
_____
_____
_____
_____
_____

Excuses are often masking a deeper concern or fear you have. To find what this is make a list below of the worst possible things that could happen once you achieve your goals.

This is the only time you can speculate on the worst!

_____
_____
_____
_____
_____
_____
_____
_____
_____
_____
_____
_____
_____
_____

Was there a pattern or common theme in these "worst case scenarios"? The common themes are the areas you need to work on to be able to eliminate excuses.

_____
_____
_____
_____
_____
_____
_____
_____
_____
_____
_____

List 3 things you will do differently to take personal responsibility and eliminate excuses in order to become more resilient, and achieve great things when faced with adversity?

_____
_____
_____
_____
_____
_____
_____
_____
_____
_____
_____
_____

*Spend high quality time with
high quality people.*

Support

The last thing you need when something has gone wrong is someone saying "I told you so", "that was never going to work" and the like. Have you had that happen to you? Was it helpful? If people do not add value to your life let them go. It sounds harsh but you cannot soar when you are weighed down by other people's negativity and their desire to keep you at their level.

This does not necessarily mean that you cut them out of your life completely, it just means that you need to choose who you let in on your goals, hopes and desires. Let in the people who will be your cheerleaders and leave out the dream stealers. It is easy to spot the dream stealers. They are the ones that will always tell you that you will never make it and they are the people who always criticise successful people. Let them steal someone else's dream, not yours.

There is a great quote that says, "leaving someone behind doesn't mean you hate them, it means you love yourself." In my life I have done just that. I left behind some people who I was very close to. I have had no contact with them since as I know that they were never going to be truly happy for me to chase the goals I had set for myself. It was a situation where any time I shared something positive in my life these people saw that as me flaunting their own failures.

When it gets to the point in a relationship where you are only comfortable sharing the things that are wrong you know it is time to move on. The saying goes that "misery loves company" and this situation was an example of this. It was difficult to do at first but it became quite liberating and made room to welcome people into my life that I could celebrate success openly without the fear that they were feeling upset or threatened by it. These people also gave great moral support when times were tougher.

> *"If everyone is moving forward together, then success takes care of itself."*
> - Henry Ford

Support can come in many forms ranging from emotional and moral support which we often get from partners, family and friends (if you have the type of family and friends that will be your cheerleaders. Sometimes it is best to find a well matched coach or mentor) through to financial and strategic support which we usually get from paid professionals.

The reality is that the more you have happening in your life, personal and professional, the more sources of support you will need to be successful. It is also true that as you become more successful, the higher you have to set your sights on the support you need in your life. You will outgrow people in your life and over time your network will evolve and change as you grow.

We become the average of the 5 people we spend most of our time with. If these 5 people are ambitious, then you are likely to be ambitious. If they are generous, then you are likely to be generous. If they happen to be lazy and negative, then you guessed it, you are likely to also be negative and lazy.

Take a moment to think about the 5 people

you spend most of your time with. There is an exercise at the end of this section to "audit" your top 5. Write their names down and a couple of qualities about them that stand out – strengths or weaknesses. Are you happy to be the average of them? If not, make a list of the qualities you want to have personally that will help you achieve the life you desire and write down people that have these qualities.

Bring people into your life that you want to become like and spend more time with them. There is a saying that goes, "If you want to be a millionaire, hang out with billionaires". Keep this in mind when thinking about who you want to learn from. This does not mean you have to physically spend time with them. It can be the programs you listen to or it could be the books you read. Always be focused on quality information and energy coming into your life.

When I wanted to be a speaker, I sought out one of the best to learn from and that was Pat Mesiti. I read his books, listened to his audios and attended his training to receive personal mentoring from him. What started with Pat now has me speaking for a living in a relatively short period of time. When I wanted to learn specific speaking skills beyond the initial learnings, I sought out speakers who specialised in those skills. Having mentors shortcuts your path to success.

Now as my business grows, not everyone around me understands my level of commitment and ambition. To help with this I have sought out a great group of business advisers who also have brought together an amazing community of vibrant entrepreneurs who have become an extremely important part of my world and my results and higher sights are reflecting this.

Aligning yourself with people and organisations that share your values and philosophies will have a great impact on your ability to keep focused on your vision when it is tested.

When something goes wrong seek out those who will encourage and support you. Hopefully these people are already close to you. Consider finding the help from someone who has overcome a similar problem to mentor you to get you back on track in the quickest way possible. They are the best qualified to advise you, and the time and the money you may need to invest in their help is nothing compared to how they will accelerate your success.

"You need to be aware of what others are doing, applaud their efforts, acknowledge their successes, and encourage them in their pursuits. When we all help one another, everybody wins."
-Jim Stovall

Support in Action

What are some signs that you might need to leave someone behind and write about a time you have left someone behind who was not providing you with positive support?

List some of your strengths that you could use to support others?

Your "Top 5 Audit"

Name	Positive Traits	Negative	Top 5 Worthy?

Goal	Support Required/Desired

Improvisation

A while ago, my husband Mike, his son Jett and I were heading off to spend the afternoon with a friend and her kids at Goolwa. Goolwa is a beautiful little town where the Murray River meets the coast in SA. It has great beaches and is on a lovely stretch of the river. It is a beautiful spot for a summer afternoon and we had an absolutely cracker day weather wise for it. We had loaded the car with all of our gear and headed off. It is a beautiful drive from where we live in the Adelaide Hills to Goolwa and I was daydreaming looking out the window watching the gorgeous countryside go by on the way.

> *"If you hit a wrong note, then make it right by what you play afterwards."*
> -Joe Pass

About an hour later we pulled into their yard and they came out to greet us with hugs and kisses all round, and the kids were quick to catch up with each other. It was the usual routine for me as I started to get out of the car while Mike got my wheelchair from boot and put it together for me. A few moments later Mike came to my door with a look of dread on his face… He'd left my wheelchair in the carport at home!

In a split second I had a decision to make on how I was going to react. I could have gotten angry and blamed Mike for forgetting it, even though it is my chair and the responsibility lies solely on me (I am just grateful that in all the years we've been together it has only happened twice – the other time was much closer to home though!); I could have sulked about it, gone home and either picked up the chair and headed back down or just stayed home; or I could challenge my improvisation skills and find a way to still make a day of it. Well the first thing I did was burst out laughing. I thought it was hysterically funny. So did my friend and the kids. The only person stony faced was Mike because he was so embarrassed. I also quickly shared it with my friends on Facebook. They thought it was funny too! We thought quickly and came up with a plan to park our car next to the barbecue so I could stay in the car but still be close to everyone. It took a bit of musical cars to clear a path but it was a great move. I opened the car door, grabbed a drink and was still very involved in getting lunch ready even though I was sitting in the car. When it was time to eat we found a dining chair with arms and I improvised my way out of the car and into the chair. I had never done anything like it before but hey, it was all part of the adventure.

After lunch I jumped back into the car and we drove down by the river and I chatted to my friend while watching Mike and the kids canoeing. It ended up being a great day and even better than I had thought it would be. Everyone had a good time and most of us had a laugh, a stark contrast to how the day could have turned out if I chose not to see it as an adventure and improvise.

As a speaker and trainer, the ability to improvise has been a huge asset for me. Every event and audience is so different that I cannot just expect everything will be as smooth as the event before. Interruptions, questions that take the flow of conversation in a different direction or an event running late and being asked to cut my session short are just a few of the challenges encountered that have required me to improvise and "think on my feet". Pun intended!

The funny thing is that when things don't go according to plan and you have to think quickly, often an even better way of doing things is discovered. This is exactly how chocolate chip cookies came to be. In the 1930s, when Ruth Wakefield was mixing a batch of her cookies she discovered she ran out of bakers' chocolate. She decided to break up a block of sweetened chocolate and add it to the mix thinking it would melt through. Instead the pieces stayed in small chunks and chocolate chip cookies were born.

> *"I'll play it first and tell you what it's called later".*
> -Miles Davis

The best thing about improvising when things don't go according to plan is that it really does not matter if it does not work. You have not invested a lot of time and energy into an outcome. You have probably improvised hundreds of times before and not even been aware of it.

The beauty is now that you are aware that something going wrong does not mean game over, you will be able to spot the opportunities for improvising. Sometimes these improvisations can have incredible results. The more you do it the better you will get at it. Rather than get weighed down by looking at every possibility, just take some action. Doing something is better than doing nothing at all.

Sometimes opportunities pop up that you are not ready for. When this happens most of the time they get dismissed. In these situations, if it is in alignment with your vision and values, say yes. You can figure out the rest later. You do not have to always know exactly how you are going to do it. More often than not the fear of not being good enough kicks in and tries to prevent you taking action. You can override that by just taking some action to get started no matter how insignificant the action may seem at the time. Once started momentum takes over and you are on your way.

Sometimes it can be an idea that pops into your mind out of nowhere. Rather than analyse it to the ^{n}th degree, just be grateful for the idea and use it.

Improvisation in Action

Think about a time where things did not turn out as planned. You surprised yourself and they actually turned out better. Write about what you did when plans went off track that led to a more positive outcome.

Think of an opportunity you were really excited about but did not know how you would make it work which you turned down. Now imagine that you said yes, even without knowing how to make it work. Write down 3 possible actions you could have taken to just get started.

"Whatever words we utter should be chosen with care for people will hear them and be influenced by them for good or ill".
-Buddha

Language

One of the easiest ways to get things back on track when something goes wrong is to change the language we use in conversations with others and in our own thoughts. Whenever possible emphasise the positive and take the attention off the negative. Too often people exaggerate the negative. I refer to this as "awfulising" a situation.

Here are a few scenarios that people would quite often refer to as being devastated by:

You are ready for an important meeting, a meeting that you have spent a lot of time preparing for. You get to the meeting, set up the projector and reach into your pocket only to discover that you left your USB memory stick with your presentation loaded on it at home;

Your favourite football team has made the Grand Final. You are all dressed up in your club colours and head off to the game. They are leading at half time and playing strong then with 10 minutes to go, a refereeing decision goes against them and as a result the other team score points and run away with a win;

A very close lifelong friend of yours dies suddenly.

Clearly the only scenario that is genuinely devastating is the death of someone close to you. Forgetting the USB stick is inconvenient and your team losing is disappointing. Neither of those is devastating. It is great that people like to widen their vocabulary and use emotive words but there is a time and place for the truly negative and dark ones.

The words you use have the power to build up or tear down the people you are dealing with or in the case of your thoughts they can pick you up or drag you down.

When it comes to the processes ticking over in your own thoughts, I have noticed that there are 3 things that people commonly say that hold them back.

I know

Have you ever heard or read something and said to yourself "yeah I know that", then disregarded the information? You are likely missing out on learnings you really need. A better question to ask is "am I doing this?" There is a big difference between knowing and implementing. Would you agree? Often you need to see the same information in many different ways before you start using it.

Should

The word should is one of the most disempowering words I have ever encountered. Usually used to beat yourself up for not doing something (e.g., "I really should have done that"), or to convince yourself to do something you really do not want to do (e.g., "I should do that now"), the whole energy of the word is deflating. Do not even get me started about when someone says "You should do that"!! If this awful word does get under your radar try interchanging it with will if it is about something in the future or if it is about something you have not done try saying could have instead.

What if?

When deciding whether or not to take action

on an idea your brain often goes into an overload of "what if?" questions. The problem is that most of the questions are relating to the possibility of something going wrong, "what if I lose my money?", "what if no-one likes it?", "what if I get hurt?"

When you feel these questions creeping in flip them on their head and ask "what if it does work?", "what if it makes loads of money?", "what if it changes people's lives in an amazing way?" Change the focus to set an intention of a positive outcome.

It all comes down to asking better quality questions.

Make a game out of finding the most uplifting angle you can on your words. In a session I was running for a client on R U OK? Day, I got people into pairs and asked them to practice responding to being asked "how are you?" in the most positive way they could. The best response was orgasmic! How does it get any better than that?

"Handle them carefully, for words have more power than atom bombs".
-Pearl Strachan

People have become accustomed to "How are you?" just being part of a greeting with no desire to hear the answer. By throwing something super positive and different at them you will spark their interest. On the flipside, if you have people in your life who are perpetual complainers do not even ask the question!

Practise censoring yourself as you are speaking. Take a moment to consider what you are going to say and aim to say it with a more positive spin. When you start doing this you will become incredibly aware of the language that other people use, and while it isn't appropriate to correct them, by paraphrasing what they say back to them in a subtle but more positive way it is amazing how quickly you can turn a conversation around.

Digging for the positive in everything you do will help you to stay focused and have a clear head to tackle finding a solution to the problem that is holding you up. It will also bring positive people and opportunities into your life via the Law Of Attraction. People will be drawn to your energy and attitude.

The other danger when it comes to language is saying things sarcastically or in jest and what that can lead to. I learned this the hard way when I was competing at the Australian Athletics Championships. Being quite new to athletics, I was still using a beginner type racing wheelchair which was double the weight of most competitor's chairs and it had terrible steering. I christened the chair the "shopping trolley". I joked about the 100m being over too fast so I would make it last a little longer. I joked about my opposition making me a cup of tea while they were waiting at the finish line for me to finish the race and I was paranoid about the steering on the chair.

Come race time the grandstand was packed and it was freezing cold with a fierce headwind. The starters' gun went and we were off. My opposition quickly finished and I was going pretty well. Until half way down the straight my chair started veering to the left. The problem here was I could only steer left! I looked at how far away the finish line was and saw that the inside rail was going to come faster. I ended up against the inside rail and thought I could force the chair along the rail to the finish line.

Unfortunately, the chair got stuck. All of the eyes in the grandstand were on me. I did not feel them though. I had created my own bubble and it was me and the finish line. In that moment I decided that what was happening was funny, not embarrassing and would make for a good story. Fortunately, I am the resilience expert! With a little extra effort I was able to pop up the front wheel and straighten the chair up which was met with a loud cheer from the crowd and I finished the race. I could not get out of the chair fast enough.

The reality was that the whole situation was manifested by the jokes I was making before the race. You see the universe does not get tone or sarcasm, it just hears the actual words. The funniest thing that came of it was that I was listed on the International Paralympic Committee World rankings for my classification as doing the 100m in 2 minutes 27 seconds! The rest of the world now thinks I am no threat which means I can fly under the radar and blow them away in future events.

*"Keep your thoughts positive
because your thoughts become your words.
Keep your words positive
because your words become your behaviour.
Keep your behaviour positive
because your behaviour becomes your habits.
Keep your habits positive
because your habits become your values.
Keep your values positive
because your values become your destiny."*
–M.K. Gandhi

Language in Action

How do you usually react to a setback or something going wrong? What is your initial reaction and your reaction as time goes by. What things do you say? How do you react physically? How do you feel?

How do you usually respond when asked "How are you?" List them below and then rate on scale of 1 – 10 how positive it is (1 being most negative, 10 being most positive)

List the most positive ways to respond when asked "How are you?" Remember to use them.

Inspiration

Inspiration is our drive to achieve. It is our purpose, our vision and our big "why". When something goes wrong, revisit the purpose and reasons behind the goals you have set. Think about why you to achieve that particular goal. How will you feel when you are successful? Doing this will energise you to stay focussed on getting past any problem that may arise along your journey. Having a strong emotional connection to your vision and purpose is essential for it to drive you when things are not going as well as you had hoped.

> *"When you discover your mission, you will feel its demand. It will fill you with enthusiasm and a burning desire to get to work on it."*
> -W. Clement Stone

If like many of the people I work with, you do not have a clear why then skip ahead to the next section "Inspiration in Action" where you can go through an exercise to help uncover what really inspires you.

Like most people I had set goals for myself that I wanted to make lots of money, travel the world and never have to work for someone else. What I did not do at the time was connect with why I really wanted all of those things. What it would mean to me to have achieved them. As a result, I did not make a great deal of progress until I worked out why.

I found my purpose in 2011 after spending 2 weeks in Honiara, the capital of the Solomon Islands, at a peer to peer training camp educating local wheelchair users who had no access to rehabilitation or education about their disabilities. It was then I realised that the experiences I have had as a wheelchair user with a spinal injury, with all the good and bad that goes with it, could help to educate and inspire wheelchair users in developing countries to have a better quality of life and to stay alive.

I was able to give them information, as well as encouragement to be active members of their communities and get involved in Disabled People's Organisations. I encouraged them to start to change the environment and attitudes that have prevented them from having any level of participation previously. All of that felt amazing.

This experience had a life changing effect on me. I had never been overseas before, certainly not to a developing country where the conditions were so oppressive. The growth I experienced was a revelation. It gave me strength to further my desire to get out and achieve great things in my life in order to raise awareness of the issues people with disabilities in developing countries face, to free up my own time and money to work in other countries of need and in indigenous communities in remote Australia.

Closer to home, I am inspired and energised by connecting with audiences at speaking engagements, by people I have not met yet but connected with online who share how they have been impacted by hearing or reading some of the lessons I have learned. Experiencing how people open up and share after I have been authentic and vulnerable inspires me to do more to create that shift in others.

On a business level, I am inspired to engage

with organisations that are going through tough and uncertain times, to inspire their people to see the opportunity in change and adversity. It excites me to help open their eyes to the influence they can have if they engage in the process of change rather than just sitting back and complaining about what is happening "to them". I personally push myself beyond my comfort zones in sport and business to help inspire others to push themselves beyond what they feel they are capable of too.

Now that I have my purpose and a very clear vision of it I can keep moving when things go wrong. All I need to do is take myself back to the trip to Solomon Islands, to the connections I have made, the impact those experiences had on me and sit with how that feels and my inspiration is recharged. Make sure you are clear on your "why" so you can use it to recharge your inspiration too.

*"A difficult time can be more readily endured
if we retain the conviction that
our existence holds a purpose
- a cause to pursue, a person to love,
a goal to achieve."*
-John Maxwell

Inspiration in Action

Not everyone has discovered their life's purpose. In some cases people thought they had only to find they had outgrown it or life had changed in a way that what was once a powerful motivator now holds little spark. Even if you feel completely connected to your purpose the series of questions on next page are great to consider.

Often my clients go through these and are excited that they confirm what they were considering. Others are surprised that something they give little credit to is actually their greatest gift to the world. Either way, take time to go through these questions and reflect on what comes up for you.

**Meditate/connect and ask these questions –
trust your intuition and the first thing that comes to mind.**

What do you think about every day?

_____
_____
_____
_____
_____
_____
_____
_____
_____
_____
_____

What are you passionate about?

_____
_____
_____
_____
_____
_____
_____
_____
_____
_____
_____

What do you talk about a lot?

What are you good at?

What do other people ask for your opinion and advice about?

What do you see in the world you wish you could change?

If time and money posed no barrier what would you do each day?

When do you feel most energised and alive? What are you doing?

What do you feel drawn towards? What are you most curious about?

Be selfish and forget about the rest of the world for a moment. Think about who you really are inside, not what you show the rest of the world. What are the differences? How will connecting with your purpose help to bring out who you really are for the rest of the world to see?

Using the answers to the questions above, create a personal "vision statement". Write this, print it, make it "you" and reflect on it morning and night.

Expand

Expand the world of others by giving. Giving time. Giving money. Giving both. Some people are in a position to give their time as they do not have a lot of money but they do have some time on their hands while others have a lot more money but are time poor. Both scenarios provides great benefit to those it provides assistance to and it feels wonderful to be in a position to have a positive impact on someone that is less fortunate than you. By expanding the world of others, you are in turn expanding your own world.

"Volunteers aren't paid, not because they are worthless, but because they are priceless."

I found this to be personally true when I was spending time one-on-one with some of the people at the peer-to-peer training camp in the Solomon Islands. Sharing my own personal experiences and providing mentoring to the participants was amazing. Being vulnerable and honest gave the participants the confidence to open up and share too. These times of mutually sharing allowed issues to be discussed that were off our agenda but were of great importance to their wellbeing.

Coming home after that trip, my world felt massively expanded. My job and life felt so tiny and insignificant in comparison. This feeling has driven me now to give more and more.

Helping others is also one of the quickest ways to take the focus off what is going wrong in your own life. While helping someone else solve their problems you quite often find the answer to your own. How often have you found yourself discussing someone else's problem and you've had an "a-ha" moment that has been as much a benefit to them as it was for yourself?

Share what you know and do it abundantly. Some people are so fearful of loss that they keep everything they know to themselves. When you help others to achieve their goals, they will be keen to assist you in any way they can to achieve your own goals. Napoleon Hill shared this in his book Think and Grow Rich when he said, "it is literally true that you can succeed best and quickest by helping others to succeed." Do not let your own expectations be the reason you help others! Helping others without expectation is what is rewarding.

When giving so abundantly and openly be sure that you do not neglect your own needs. Balance between giving and receiving is a must. Women are particularly prone to selflessly devoting themselves to helping others, especially when they become mothers while neglecting making time to ensure their own needs are being fulfilled. There is a tendency towards putting children first, then partners and work. As a result they feel guilty, become overwhelmed and burnt out. Making time for yourself is not selfish. It is essential. The more fulfilled and nourished you are, the greater your capacity to give to others.

Constantly expand your own knowledge, skills and experiences. Some people prefer to learn in a structured way such as through university or vocational courses, others prefer to learn through experiencing new things or by reading or listening to books. Think about the ways you most prefer to learn. How much time are you dedicating to expanding yourself? At a minimum set aside 30 mins per day for your self-education.

Seek ways to expand your networks and in turn to expand the networks of those around you. When speaking to people be present and listen carefully for opportunities where you may be able to connect them with another person in your network that would be mutually beneficial. I was excited to see the opportunity to introduce two of my sponsors to each other. They provide great support to my sporting endeavours, are located geographically close by and share a similar client-base so it made sense to see how they could work together.

"Thousands of candles can be lighted from a single candle, and the life of the candle will not be shortened. Happiness never decreases by being shared."
–Buddha

Expansion in Action

What do you think of when you hear the word "expansion"?

___

Looking at your "Vision Statement" created in the previous chapter, list ways you can "expand" yourself in order to get closer to achieving your vision

___

Again referring to your vision statement, list ways you can "expand" others and the world around you

_____
_____
_____
_____
_____
_____
_____

Look at the lists you have made of ways to expand yourself and to expand others.

List 3 below that you would like to do in your life now

_____
_____
_____
_____
_____
_____
_____

List 3 below that you would like to do in your life if time and money was no barrier

_____
_____
_____
_____
_____
_____
_____

Next

Always have your focus firmly set on what the next immediate task is, not what has already been done. Getting weighed down in what has happened will make it difficult to focus on finding a solution to the problem at hand. Think clearly about the next action, not a series of actions down the track or the series of actions that have gone before.

This key highlights the importance of good planning and goal setting. If you have planned well, you will know exactly what the next step is that you need to get to after where things have not gone to plan. This means you have something smaller and within reach to aim for rather than just the big end result. It will make it easier to find a way to get to that next step. Without a plan it can be overwhelming.

I plan my day but not to the minute as I like to have some flexibility to work in a way that is guided by my energy and intuition. This works well for me when things are going smoothly, but when things go wrong the plan keeps much of the emotion from the equation and allows me to stay in action.

When it comes to goal setting most people have been taught the S.M.A.R.T. goal setting system. This system dictates that a goal is to be Specific, Measurable, Achievable, Relevant and Timely. This model has served many people well and it is a great place to start when setting your goals. The area I always advise people to stretch themselves with is the "achievable" criteria. There is a risk here of people playing it too safe. Who knows what you are capable of if your desire is strong enough? Tie everything in to your vision and purpose. One of my previous mentors drummed into me the saying "if the dream is big enough the facts don't matter."

Balance your goal setting with having some very big long term goals that really stretch you mixed in with lots of shorter term easier to achieve goals. Achieving these smaller goals is a good motivator to keep working towards the big ones. Nothing breeds success like success!

However you decide to do your goal setting activities make sure you put them in writing. As well as writing the words, you can create visual references to them using photos, drawings or video. Committing them to paper is the first step to committing them to the world. Have you ever written out your goals, then found the piece of paper years later to find that you have been able to tick many of them off the list? Once you have them in writing refer to them daily and use them to create your actions.

While putting them to paper is a start, you do need to take action to make them happen and keep you focussed, especially under pressure. Once you have the goals written down, write down the processes you need to do repeatedly to achieve the goal. For example, if you wanted to lose a certain amount of weight by a certain date you would need to eat a specific way every day and do a specific amount of physical activity every day. When your focus is on what you need to do each day, it makes achieving the goal much easier.

> "If you don't know where you are going, you'll end up someplace else."
> -Yogi Berra

Accountability is an important tool for staying on track with your goals and actions, especially when things don't go to plan. Having a coach or mentor to assist you with the clarity to know what to do next has been an asset for me. You cannot have your partner, family or your best friend do this for you. It needs to be someone completely impartial who won't accept the excuses that come up along the way.

Things are bound to go wrong. Even though each time feels like a failure it isn't permanent. Michael Jordan summed it up perfectly when he said, "I've failed over and over and over again in my life, and that is why I succeed." Each time things go wrong look for the lesson in it. Also look at it as a great way of testing how good your goal setting and planning is. If you have planned well, it will not take long at all to get yourself working on the next action.

More often than not, things will deviate from the original plan for success. Persistence needs to be in plentiful supply, it is almost like the universe throws curve balls at us to test us to see how strong our desire to succeed is. Having persistence is the difference between giving up when you reach a dead-end and digging out your maps to find the detour back to the place where you will be back on the right track to the goal you are working towards.

It is much easier to be persistent when you know what the next task is! If in doubt, just do something. Sitting idle allows your brain to go into "awfulising" mode. Do not give it the chance. You are more powerful than that. The longer you leave it, the harder it is to get moving again. There is no defying the law of inertia.

Conquer it with momentum and remember that small wins attract big wins.

> *"Our plans miscarry because they have no aim.
> When a man does not know what harbor he is making for,
> no wind is the right wind."*
> —Seneca

Next in Action

How do you set and record your goals?

Which aspects of your current goal setting processes work well?

Which aspects of your current goal setting processes would you like to improve?

Looking back over the past year think about the goals you set and have not yet achieved. What has held you back from achieving them and how do you feel about it?

What do you do daily to get you closer to your goal (i.e., what are the processes required repeatedly to achieve your goal)?

_____
_____
_____
_____
_____
_____

How do you remain accountable to your goals?

_____
_____
_____
_____
_____
_____
_____
_____
_____
_____

How connected do you feel your goals are to your vision?

_____
_____
_____
_____
_____
_____
_____
_____
_____
_____

"Procrastination is opportunity's assassin. "
-Victor Kiam

Time

We do not have an infinite supply of time, therefore, it is important to make every minute count. Ask yourself "is what I am doing right now what I need to be doing to get closer to my vision and to solve the problem at hand?" It is much easier to do everything but address the problem. Believe me there have been many times when I have cleaned the house, rearranged cupboards and played games when I could have been finding solutions.

Another question to ask yourself if you feel procrastination setting in is "what am I really putting off?" Each and every time you procrastinate you are pushing your dream further and further away. Christopher Parker said, "Procrastination is like a credit card: it's a lot of fun until you get the bill." So true!

Procrastination not only delays the achievement of our goals, it can lead to other bigger problems in our lives. On one end of the scale, it can lead to a sense of apathy and laziness, killing our desire to succeed. On the other end of the scale, it can lead to high levels of stress, anxiety and panic especially when a deadline is fast approaching. This is where I found myself most of the time. I even justified it by telling everyone that I produced my best work when under pressure. Somehow I always managed to pull it off at the last minute and I kept doing it. The reality is that you just work faster with a deadline, not differently. Think about how much you get done in the days before you go on holidays. There is no reason that you can't work like that all of the time.

I actually branded myself the Queen of Procrastination. Back in the days of MySpace it was even my personal tag line. That was until I read Napoleon Hill's *Think and Grow Rich* and learned that mastery of procrastination was an essential step to success. Here I was wondering why my goals were not being realised when it was largely because of my damaging habit of procrastinating. Needless to say I was no longer proud of my former title and I have left it behind forever. The progress I have made towards the life I dream of is a reflection of transitioning from being the Queen of Procrastination to the Queen of Productivity!

Have you got a project you can never seem to finish? Do you have a habit of starting lots of things but not seeing them through to completion? Perhaps you are so much of a procrastinator that you do not even get started? I fell into the 3 categories above too and it frustrated me because I could not work out why. At first I thought it was lack of clarity and poor planning. Now I know it is a tricky little thing we encounter called "Resistance". The place it has been most apparent in my life has been around finishing this book. At the time I am writing this I am already 9 months behind schedule and it was not until I read "Do The Work" by Steven Pressfield that I understood why In this book I discovered how resistance manifests itself in your life in the form of procrastination and what you can do to conquer it. Resistance is particularly strong when it comes to entrepreneurs and creative types but the principle affects everyone.

What we do with our time plays a huge role in the progress we make towards our goals and as discussed in the previous key "Next Action" planning our tasks is critical. Essentially, there is no such thing as Time Management as it is impossible for us to manage time. What we can do is manage our behaviour and what we do with the time we have. How often do we and those around us complain about not having enough time? The reality is that if we carefully analyse what we do hour to hour we have a lot of time.

The founder of IKEA, Ingvar Kamprad, took this a step further when he famously said, "Ten minutes are not just one-sixth of your hourly pay; ten minutes is a piece of yourself. Divide yourself into ten units and sacrifice as few of them as possible in meaningless activities." We just need to be productive instead of merely being busy. Busy does not get things done. Having high levels of productivity gets things done.

The other aspect to time being a principle of resilience is having downtime to recharge. Getting a decent amount of sleep each night is very important as being tired is a definite way to reduce your productivity levels. It is best to go to bed early and get up early as the quality of sleep is better early in the night. The great thing about getting up early is that most people do not so you get some distraction free time in the early hours.

It is a real balancing act to find the right proportion of leisure time to productive time. Depending on the tasks at hand that time will vary greatly. It took me a long time to cut into my social life time to gain more productive time. In the beginning my friends and family did not understand why I spent my weekends working on projects instead of at the beach or sharing a few drinks over a barbecue. Do not get me wrong I love being social but putting in the hard work to achieve a goal makes the social time at the end of it all the more satisfying.

At 36 years old, I am still trying to find the best way of juggling 2 growing businesses and elite athlete training while having the existing challenges from disability. Not to mention somewhere in there finding the time to be a wife, friend and family member! I do not always get it right but I also don't dwell too long on beating myself up about it either. That is good for nothing. The biggest thing that has helped is being totally immersed in my vision. Make sure that you prioritise that and it will go a long way towards keeping you productive and sane.

"Much may be done in those little shreds and patches of time which every day produces, and which most men throw away."
-Charles Caleb Colton

Time in Action

What does "time management" mean to you?

How do you rate yourself in the area of productivity?

Do you find yourself procrastinating often? If so, what are your top 3 time wasters?

Do you find yourself making excuses for not getting things done? If so, what excuses do you commonly make? (Look back to the chapter on Excuses to see if these excuses came up then too and what they are really hiding)

_____
_____
_____
_____
_____
_____
_____

What 3 activities/tasks take up most of your time on a typical day? Could you delegate, outsource or just stop doing them?

_____
_____
_____
_____
_____
_____
_____

What time of the day are your energy levels at their highest? Create a plan to work on your most important tasks at this time. Your most important tasks are those that bring in revenue and are getting you closer to achieving your vision. List these below.

_____
_____
_____
_____
_____
_____

Bonus Principles

The principles shared so far were first penned a few years ago. Those 9 principles captured what got me from the despair of having my life turned upside down to where I was at that time. In the years since my life has grown in ways I never imagined possible. During this time, there have been a couple of additional principles that I have discovered that have elevated me to where I am now and are crucial to where I am heading.

After speaking to thousands of people and having so many of them share their stories and challenges with me, I have realised just how important these additional principles are.

Confidence

The word confidence itself has the tendency to leave most people shuddering. Why is it that so many people lack the confidence to step up, be the best they can and own it?

From my own experience and what I have seen in people around me, the major thing getting in people's way is fear. Oscillating between fear of failure and fear of success is where so many people find themselves, without even realising it. Fear of failure is a common barrier. People are worried about losing money, about being publicly embarrassed, about what other people think of them. Recognising the fear of success is not often a conscious thought.

One of the biggest mistakes made when it comes to confidence is looking at other people and comparing yourself to them. While there seems to be an illusion of having it all together and doing fabulously, you must consider what is happening below that exterior. Some people do well to put on a cool and calm public face while things behind the scenes are in disarray. It is like looking at a duck or a swan gliding along a lake. What we can't see is their little legs paddling furiously below the surface.

I was so surprised that time and time again when taking questions at presentations I was doing or when working one-on-one with clients that the people I saw as successful and in control were the ones asking for advice on confidence. What I noticed was that these people would down play their achievements, worried that they did not deserve the accolades they received and they felt like a fraud. I too was one of those people who looked like I had it all together but inside was a nervous mess and also felt like a fraud, especially in two of the situations that most people are scared of, specifically public speaking and striking up conversations with strangers.

When I first started speaking I was determined that I was not going to talk about myself. I wanted to speak to raise awareness and money to work more with people with disability in developing countries. Talking about an issue or other people felt more comfortable because it protected me from being personally judged. I was worried if I did speak about my personal story and experiences that I would come across as conceited or arrogant. The Tall Poppy Syndrome has a lot to answer for!

Thankfully I had the benefit of doing my earliest speaker training with Pat Mesiti who quickly quashed those thoughts. He clearly articulated that speaking is not about the speaker. It is about the audience and the benefit an audience receives from hearing the stories and experiences of a speaker. Shifting that perception from myself to the fact that everyone in an audience wants me to do well and they see me as having the answers they need to address their personal challenges set up sharing my story to be a far more empowering experience than I was initially thinking.

There were still doubts about how valuable my experiences were to someone else. The "Little Old Me Syndrome". How on Earth could my life impact anyone else, I was thinking. Again I was fortunate to have Pat step in and bluntly tell me that my story had value, not just for people who had faced the same challenges, but to people in the business world and beyond that I would be incredibly selfish not to share. How can you argue with that? Without that conversation it is unlikely that I would be sharing this with you now. Thanks Pat.

Once I started speaking and sharing my story I found how being open and vulnerable gave me the ability to connect with others. As I began to appreciate the value in doing this and truly believe in myself, my message and my confidence grew, as did my business. Discovering who I authentically am and loving that person was transformational. The realisation that I get paid to be myself was mind blowing.

> *"Believe in yourself! Have faith in your abilities! Without a humble but reasonable confidence in your own powers you cannot be successful or happy."*
> ~ Norman Vincent Peale

Confidence comes from being truly authentic and living in alignment with that. It also comes from being honest about what you really want in your life. It comes from within and from clarity. Being clear about your vision for your life is not arrogant, nor is being clear on your own ability and capacity. Certainty builds confidence as does improving competence.

The easiest was to feel and appear confident in situations where you need to interact with people you do not know (the ability to have conversations with strangers is a crucial skill to succeed in business and in life) is to lead the conversation and make it all about the other person. Having a stock of questions to keep a conversation centred on others takes the pressure off you and the reality is that most people love speaking about themselves! They will go away thinking that you are awesome when they really do not know that much about you other than that you are a good listener.

Make people feel that they are important by being genuinely interested in them and you will go a long way towards establishing lasting relationships. However, you need to make sure that the relationships do not end up being completely one sided. You will know soon enough which ones are worth the effort and which ones are not.

It does not matter how successful you become, the voice of doubt will still pay regular visits in your head. Eckhart Tolle in his book "A New Earth" has a great insight on how to deal with this. He says to acknowledge the voice and that you are not the voice. You are aware of the voice. Look for the fact in the story it is telling you. For example, you may be hearing, "everything is hopeless". The fact in that may be that you only have 50 cents in your bank account. A story limits you from taking action whereas a fact can empower you to take action. Do not get caught up in those stories! I find when those voices pay me a visit I have a quick conscious word with them. I say, "Thanks for your concern, I appreciate you looking out for me but I have got this." Trying to ignore the voices is futile they do not go away. If they are being particularly stubborn I dig out testimonials and feedback forms from past clients and read how much of an impact I had. Tackle the voices head on, then move on.

Do not let what you believe you are capable of in this moment determine the bigness of the goal you set for yourself in the future. Aim high.

You can learn how to become the person you need to be to achieve those goals. Whenever you set goals for yourself take a moment to ask, how much bigger can I make this? If the thought of your goal does not give you butterflies in your stomach it is not big enough yet.

---

*"You gain strength, courage and confidence by every experience in which you really stop to look fear in the face. You are able to say to yourself, '
I have lived through this horror. I can take the next thing that comes along.' You must do the thing you think you cannot do."*
~ Eleanor Roosevelt

Confidence in Action

Create a notebook or online collection of all of your positive feedback from colleagues and clients. Start by making a list below of the people you have this feedback from.

_____
_____
_____
_____

Research awards to enter and fill in the nomination forms. Make a list below of the awards you find and the date nominations close.

_____
_____
_____
_____

List situations you would normally avoid. Make a time to get out and take part in them. Put them into your calendar. Remember the duck and act confident. When you get back home after each of these events take the time to journal your experiences, taking note of what you felt and observed.

_____
_____
_____
_____
_____
_____
_____

Create a collection of questions to engage people in conversation. The more they do the talking the less nervous you will be.

Make a list of people you consider extremely confident. Read and watch interviews with them, read their biographies if available to get insights into their thought processes. If you can, spend time with them and learn more about how they feel.

Not everyone has discovered their life's purpose. In some cases people thought they had only to find they had outgrown it or life had changed in a way that what was once a powerful motivator now holds little spark. Even if you feel completely connected to your purpose the series of questions in the Inspiration section are worth revisiting.

Enjoyment

To most this is going to sound obvious. The reality is when getting swept up in the day to day, it is easy to lose sight of what you really enjoy. When you enjoy what you do you are enthusiastic, motivated and look forward to it each and every day. Being in that zone means that you get excited about the alarm going off in the morning rather than groaning and wishing for more sleep.

The best thing about being in a place of inspired enjoyment is that when things do go wrong, and there is no place immune from it, you are in a position to turn what others fear into a joyous experience.

You enjoy the challenges.

You enjoy finding lessons in every day.

You enjoy finding ways to add value to the experiences of others.

In order to get to this place you need to know exactly what it is you enjoy. This is not the time to be concerned with what you believe other people might want you to say. It is 100% what you love and desire deep within yourself. It is a very personal thing and it will change as your life evolves. Be sure to check in regularly to make sure that you are still doing what makes you inspired and happy as well as working towards something that you will be fulfilled by and enjoy.

Have a bank of things you enjoy doing that you can do anywhere, anytime. When you feel like things are getting overwhelming, take a 30 minute break to do one of those things to re-energise yourself. My favourite is to get outside, soak up some sunshine and big deep breaths of fresh air. This resets my equilibrium and I am ready to forge ahead once more. Capture a list of yours in the activities at the end of this section.

When you are enjoying yourself, your energy becomes limitless and people are drawn to you. The energy you project is contagious so be conscious of where your energy is. This is especially important if you are leading and managing others. If you are not pleased with the energy and attitude of your team, make sure you check yours first before addressing theirs. When you find this happening frequently, it is time to question how much pleasure you are getting from what you are doing. You spend so much time at work or your business that you need to make sure it has a positive impact on your energy and enjoyment. As Michael Korda said, "Your chances of success are directly proportional to the degree of pleasure you desire from what you do. If you are in a job you hate, face the fact squarely and get out."

I found myself in that situation a few years back. My lack of enthusiasm for what I was doing was weighing heavily on me. You know it has become toxic when you wake up feeling less than 100% and get excited that you could call in sick. Needless to say, once I shifted myself out of that situation into one where I was in charge and responsible for the ultimate success or otherwise of my business, I thrived. If that ever happens again I'll recognise and address it a lot earlier.

When you love something you make it happen, even if it means taking risks and getting uncomfortable. Doing this started at a young age for me. When I was just shy of three years old Mum sat me in front of the television to watch Sesame Street while she hung the washing out. I had better ideas though. I wanted to go to playgroup. It was not playgroup day but that did not matter to me. I walked straight out the door and started making my way, alone and on foot to playgroup.

This was a busy suburb of Sydney and little me wandered across roads heavy with traffic and people. I was almost there when a lady noticed me and took me to the nearest police station. I cannot begin to imagine my mother's distress when she discovered I was missing. Of course, that did not cross my mind. My focus was clearly only on getting to my desired destination. Although I did not get there, holding court at the police station was pretty exciting and by the time Mum got there I was wearing a police hat, drinking milk and eating cookies. Three decades later little has changed. I know what I love, where I want to go and have clear focus on the destination. Although, now I do things in a way that won't land me at the local police station!

Be balanced in your outlook on life. While it is important to be excited about the future you are creating, take time to be mindful and enjoy the present too as it is easy to get swept up in your big plans for the future. Enjoying where you are right now and bringing your best self to every moment will give you limitless capacity to create and to connec t, which will bring those big plans to life before your eyes.

*"Learn to enjoy every minute of your life.
Be happy now.
Don't wait for something outside of yourself
to make you happy in the future.
Think how really precious is the time
you have to spend, whether it's at work or with your family.
Every minute should be enjoyed and savoured."*
~ Earl Nightingale

Enjoyment in Action

Make a list of things you enjoy where time and money pose no barrier

_____
_____
_____
_____
_____
_____
_____
_____
_____
_____

Make a list of things you enjoy that can be done anywhere, any time in 30 minutes or less

_____
_____
_____
_____
_____
_____
_____
_____
_____
_____
_____
_____

Schedule 3 things from the list above into your calendar each week, starting from this week ahead and make them non-negotiable

Summary

It has been fantastic sharing these 9 principles to being resilient with you. If you use these to develop you own personal resilience getting great results when things go wrong will become effortless. They have changed my life and they can change yours too.

You may have noticed that the first letter of each principle spells out the word **RESILIENT** which will help you to remember the principles with ease.

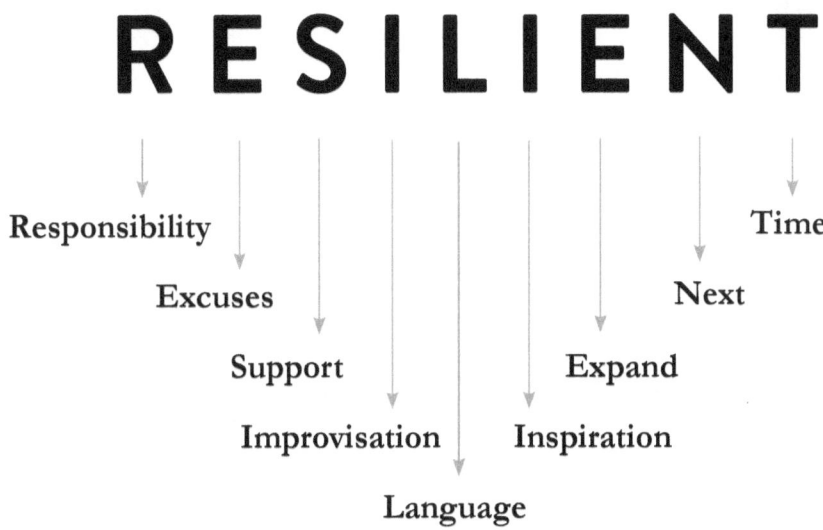

Be sure to check out the next section which will show you how you can further develop your resilience skills.

Next Steps

How are you feeling after journeying your way through what I have shared about my life, experiences, challenges and victories, and how I got from the challenges to the victories?

I realise that I have shared a lot of great content with you. I hope that you are feeling that it is content that will make a difference in your life and you can go and apply it straight away. I am also aware that there may be a tendency to feel a little overwhelmed by it all, and feel uncertain as to how to implement this in your life with your unique challenges, and desires to get results in your life quickly and easily.

By giving you the content here I have only scratched the surface of what is possible for you in your life. Information is just part of the big picture of success. What I can do for you is take you by the hand and guide you through the maze from where you are now to where you would like to be in the future.

We have all started out to achieve goals, with high levels of motivation and found it fizzling as time went by and having it disappearing completely short of the goal. This is where having someone in your corner, cheering you on and holding you accountable can play a massive part in achieving your goals and this is exactly what a coach can do for you.

Sometimes we need someone outside to tackle our problems with us as we are too close to deal with them objectively. I can do that for you. As you have seen throughout this book, I have experienced the highs and the lows. I can be there to keep you focused, to be your coach and cheerleader to get you to the place in your life you want to be as quickly, painlessly and effortlessly as possible.

This is why I have made myself available to be your coach. What makes me different from other coaches is that I will focus on exploring your potential, clarifying your direction and developing your resilience. I am not a whip cracking, high-fiving type of coach but I won't let you take it too easy either! Resilience will be the difference between achieving your goals and merely existing day to day.

If you feel that having me on your team to encourage and motivate you, and to build your resilience will help you to achieve all that you desire please email me at Stacey@HowToBeResilient.com with "Expression of Interest" as the subject. I will contact you with an application to do a free strategy session and discuss my coaching programs with you to see if we would be a good fit to work together. With an increasingly hectic schedule, I only coach 3 days per month. Due to this, I will only work with those who are committed to doing what it takes to succeed.

I would like to hear your thoughts, insights, questions, feedback and comments via Stacey@HowToBeResilient.com. From your feedback I will continue to create new content to ensure you are getting the resources needed to build your resilience. You never know, your question may be the beginnings of the next book.

Most importantly, please celebrate your successes! I love hearing about your progress, triumphs and breakthroughs. Please share them with me too. If you choose to see every situation as an opportunity to learn you will never be disappointed.

Be your best!

Stacey

*"You cannot teach a man anything.
You can only help him discover it within himself."*
-Galileo Galilei

Recommended Reading

These are a selection of books that I have found had the biggest impact personally over the years (in no particular order). I trust you find them helpful too.

The Charge – Brendon Burchard

Unprofessional – Jack Delosa

4 Hour Work Week – Tim Ferriss

Do The Work – Steven Pressfield

Eat That Frog – Brian Tracy

Think and Grow Rich – Napoleon Hill

Notes From A Friend – Tony Robbins

How To Have A Millionaire Mindset – Pat Mesiti

Questions Are The Answers – Allan Pease

Life In Half A Second – Matthew Michalewicz

The Values Factor – Dr John Demartini

About The Author

Stacey has not let a devastating accident that left her a quadriplegic and needing a wheelchair at 12 years old slow her down. Instead she picked up the pace achieving a wide array of things from running for parliament to training wheelchair users overseas and a long list of things in between.

Stacey has had more than her fair share of setbacks. She has used her life experience and personal philosophies to become a thought leader on resilience and finding the opportunity in change and adversity through delivering keynote speeches, training, consulting and coaching to organisations such as Telstra, the South Australian Cricket Association (SACA) and CSIRO.

Stacey has been featured in Sydney Morning Herald, The Age, Mamamia, Grazia, That's Life and Today Tonight and has shared the stage with legends in the speaking industry including Allan Pease, Amanda Gore and Pat Mesiti.

More recently Stacey has added athletics to her repertoire after 22 years of inactivity to further stretch her comfort zones and has a gold medal in 2016 Rio Paralympics firmly in her sights.

In her spare time, you are likely to find Stacey in the nearest patch of sunshine with a book recharging her solar powers.

You can read more about the themes that Stacey speaks about and reviews from previous clients at www.staceycopas.com/info

For speaking and media requests please contact Stacey directly at bookings@staceycopas.com.

*"People who soar are those who refuse to sit back,
sigh and wish things would change.
They neither complain of their lot nor passively
dream of some distant ship coming in.
Rather, they visualize in their minds t
hat they are not quitters; they will not allow
life's circumstances to push them
down and hold them under."*
-Charles Swindoll

www.ingramcontent.com/pod-product-compliance
Lightning Source LLC
Chambersburg PA
CBHW032043290426
44110CB00012B/928